CLOCKS

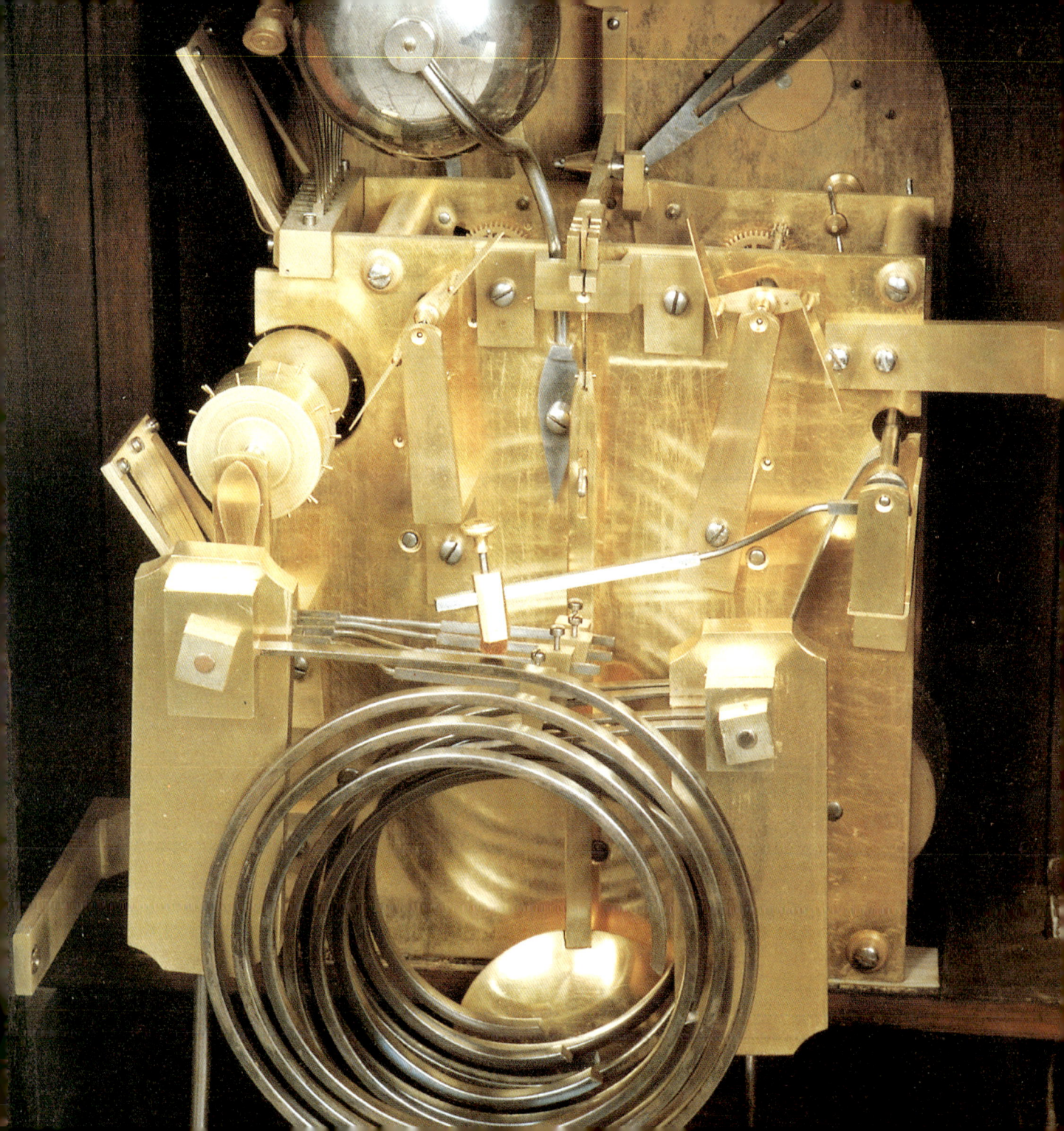

THE COLLECTOR'S CORNER

CLOCKS

A Quantum Book

Published by Grange Books
an imprint of Grange Books Plc
The Grange
Kingsnorth Industrial Estate
Hoo, nr Rochester
Kent ME3 9ND

Copyright © 1999 Quantum Books Ltd

All rights reserved.
This book is protected by copyright. No part of it may be reproduced, stored in a retrieval system, or transmitted in any form or by any means, without the prior permission in writing of the Publisher, nor be otherwise circulated in any form of binding or cover other than that in which it is published and without a similar condition
including this condition being imposed on the subsequent publisher.

ISBN 1-84013-291-4

This book is produced by
Quantum Books Ltd
6 Blundell Street
London N7 9BH

Project Manager: Rebecca Kingsley
Art Director: Siân Keogh
Project Editor: Jo Wells
Designer: Martin Laurie
Editor: Kay Macmullan

The material in this publication previously appeared in *Collecting Clocks*

QUMCCCC
Set in Gill Sans
Reproduced in Singapore by Eray Scan Pte Ltd
Printed in Singapore by Star Standard Industries (Pte) Ltd

CONTENTS

Introduction 6

American Clocks 11

English Clocks 17

Austro-Hungarian and Dutch Clocks 27

French and Swiss Clocks 33

Longcase Clocks 37

Carriage Clocks 49

Skeleton Clocks 55

Mystery, Novelty and Fantasy Clocks 61

INTRODUCTION

INTRODUCTION

• • • •

BELOW
Cleopatra's
Needle was built
in 1500 B.C.

Humans have always been aware of time and also have the ability to estimate it quite accurately. With the growth of civilization, however, our ability in this direction has gradually declined. In this way we differ from the animal kingdom, where certain types of insect have retained their sense of timing and still repeat particular actions with a variation of no more than a few seconds a day.

As civilization developed and became more sophisticated, it became necessary to denote time. The first method used was probably that of noting the position of a shadow thrown by an object such as a tree or a mountain. However, this had its draw backs and as man started to live more and more in communities, shadow clocks were erected, such as Cleopatra's Needle, the time being marked out on the ground. The next development was probably the small, portable wooden shadow clock, consisting of a horizontal bar with a raised crosspiece on one end, whose shadow would progress along the horizontal bar as the sun rose. This clock had to face east in the morning and west in the afternoon. The final and most popular development of this method of timekeeping was the garden sundial.

All these methods of determining time were fine in sunny areas such as the Middle East but would be far less practical in many other parts of the world and of no use at all in the dark of night. To overcome this problem, various other methods of telling the time were invented, such as the sandglass, in which time is

RIGHT A copy of an
early shadow clock,
dating from c8th–10th
century B.C.

6

measured by the running of sand through a narrow orifice from one container to another. Water clocks (clepsydras) based on a similar principle were also devised, and fire clocks, too, came into common use. Probably the simplest of these primitive solutions was a candle graduated down its length in hours. Other types of clock were based on the reduction of the level of oil in a lamp or the slow burning of powder along a grooved channel.

The mechanical clock

The mechanical clock, as it is known today, probably first came into being at the end of the 13th century or the beginning of the 14th century. This was made possible by the invention of the verge and foliot escapement, which works on the principle of a vertical arbor (axle) on which a horizontally oscillating bar is mounted. Flags attached to the arbor alternately stop and release the teeth of a wheel (the escape wheel), with which other wheels and pinions engage. These are then used to indicate time, usually by means of hands attached to them. The Dover Castle Clock is one of the oldest examples of a mechanical clock that retains its original verge and foliot escapement.

Many of the early clocks probably had no dial or hands but merely struck the hours. These clock were frequently made for ecclesiastical use – to call people to prayers. The earliest mechanical clocks still in existence in England today are those found in Exeter, Salisbury and Wells cathedrals. Domestic clocks did not come into use in England until

around 1600, but appeared far earlier on the Continent and in particular in southern Germany. The oldest examples of domestic clocks were weight-driven wall clocks, almost always of short duration. The invention of the coiled spring in around A.D. 1500 enabled a whole range of spring-driven table clocks to be produced, which were more portable than weight-driven clocks and were often of considerable complexity. The coiled spring also made the invention of the watch possible.

ABOVE: The Dover Castle Clock is one of the oldest clocks that still has its original verge escapement with foliot from which the regulating weights may be seen hanging.

7

INTRODUCTION

RIGHT Dating from the late 17th century, this German table clock has grande-sonnerie striking and an alarm. The case is made of fire-gilt brass.

Early watches and small spring clocks employing a balance were relatively inaccurate. It was only around the year 1670 when the hairspring, used to control the balance, was invented that the performance of such timepieces dramatically improved.

On most early turret clocks the foliot controlled timekeeping, with weights being moved, added to or removed from the bar to slow or speed it. However, on later domestic clocks, particularly the English lantern clock that started to be produced around 1600, a large balance wheel was usually preferred.

The pendulum

In the mid 17th century the pendulum was discovered, and, as a result, timekeeping was dramatically improved. It was Leonardo da Vinci who first observed that no matter how wide the arc of swing of a chandelier, the time it took to move from one side to the other always remained the same. However, it was Christiaan Huygens, the Dutch mathematician, and Salomon Coster, an eminent Dutch clockmaker, who applied the principle of the pendulum to a clock, in 1657. In a very short time this idea spread throughout Europe and in particular to England. Early pendulum clocks used a verge escapement.

German table clocks were produced from the late 16th century until well into the 18th century. The cases were of fire-gilt brass, usually either round or four-, six- or eight-sided. They were of short duration and often of considerable complexity, sometimes featuring an alarm and quite frequently being quarter-striking.

RIGHT Made in in Augsburg in southern Germany, this clock depicts the gluttonous mythical King Gambrinus, who is associated with brewing beer. On the hour, the king raises the beer mug and opens and closes his mouth.

Precision timekeeping

Man has been concerned with accurate timekeeping for at least the last millennium. The first major step towards achieving this goal came with the invention of the mechanical clock, probably in the late 13th century. The next step forward was the introduction of the pendulum in 1657, closely followed by the introduction of the anchor escapement, coupled with the royal or seconds-beating pendulum some 12 to 14 years later. Over this period clocks had improved in accuracy from an error of maybe 5–10 minutes a day to 15–20 seconds a week.

The introduction of maintaining power so that the clock did not stop while it was being wound was another step in the right direction. The first method of maintaining power was known as 'bolt and shutter', and was largely replaced in the 1730s by John Harrison's 'going ratchet'.

As the accuracy of clocks increased, the effect of changes in temperature was found to be a problem. As it got hotter the pendulum rod would expand and increase in length, thus slowing the clock. To overcome this, two principal forms of compensated pendulum were invented: the mercury-compensated pendulum and the gridiron pendulum. A mercury-compensated pendulum is one that incorporates a glass jar filled with mercury as the bob. As the rod expands down the mercury expands up, thus the leaving the length of the pendulum the same. The gridiron pendulum involves the use of a pendulum rod consisting of rods of iron and brass that are joined in such a way that their expansions cancel each other out.

Around the year 1900 a solution to this problem was found by the use of a metal known as invar, which has a negligible coefficient of expansion, for the pendulum rod. Precision clocks were also kept at constant temperatures with the aid of thermostats and electric heating. Clock movements were also kept within a sealed jar, thus preventing them being affected by any change in barometric pressure.

The final problem to be overcome on the mechanical clock (prior to its accuracy being vastly exceeded by atomic and other devices) was how to prevent the movement

LEFT This eight-day longcase regulator was made in Liverpool c1820. It was capable of keeping time to within 1–2 seconds a week.

from influencing the isochronicity (regular or even beating) of the pendulum. The ultimate solution, which took some 150 years to arrive at, was achieved by Shorn, who devised a clock with two pendulums, a 'master', which was detached from the movement and swung freely, and a 'slave', which had to do the work (it was attached to the movement).

clocks are now known as chronometers. They are contained in three-tier wooden boxes and are supported by brass gimbals, so that whatever the movement of the ship the chronometer remains horizontal. To read the time only the top lid needs to be lifted, leaving the chronometer still protected by the lower lid, which has a glazed top.

Timekeeping at sea

By the early 18th century it was realized that good timekeeping at sea was essential for accurate navigation (and also cartography). However, making a clock that could tolerate the pitching and tossing of a ship was beyond the skills and technology of any clockmaker of the time.

In order to stimulate research the British Admiralty formed a Board of Longitude which offered a prize of up to £20,000, an enormous sum in those days, to anyone who could devise a method of determining longitude at sea – in practice an accurate sea clock. One man, John Harrison (1693–1776), assisted in the early days by his brother James, worked for more than 40 years to solve this problem. His determination finally saw him receive the last part of his reward when he was nearly 80 years old.

It was left to other men such as John Arnold and Thomas Earnshaw to make Harrison's invention a reality, by simplifying its production so that it could be made in quantity without losing any of its accuracy. These sea

RIGHT
A mid-19th-century two-day, marine chronometer suspended in gimbals and contained in a three-tier brass-bound mahogany box.

CHAPTER ONE

AMERICAN CLOCKS

• • • •

Following the War of Independence in America, there was a shortage of materials and as a result a greater demand for cheaper and smaller clocks in preference to the longcase. Several clockmakers devised methods of fulfilling this demand. Backed up by the wealth of experience of immigrant clockmakers from such countries as England, The Netherlands and Germany, they designed and made clock machinery that could be easily produced by factory techniques. This avoided the expense of handcrafted production methods.

Clockmakers

Eli Terry (1772–1853) was possibly the most famous of these clockmakers, known for his successful completion of the Porter Contract, when he manufactured 4,000 complete clock movements at four dollars each over just three years. The pillar and scroll case style, together with its wooden 30-hour movement, was also developed by Eli Terry. This type of clock resulted in rapid growth of the clockmaking industry in Connecticut.

Other well-known makers who were involved in the early days of factory production were Seth Thomas, Chauncey Jerome and Simon Willard, who patented the

LEFT Produced by Eli Terry of Connecticut, this clock has three brass finials and a wooden white-painted dial. In the lower portion of the door is a reverse painting on glass of Mount Vernon, with an aperture in the centre through which the pendulum bob may be seen.

11

AMERICAN CLOCKS

RIGHT *Dating from about 1815, this banjo clock has a mahogany and gilt-wood case. The reverse-painted panel in the base depicts Perry's victory.*

banjo clock in 1802. Some had a simple box at the base, whereas others had decoration coming down below this. Many of the later examples in particular lost the quality and excellent lines of Simon Willard's original design.

Probably the finest of the early banjo clocks was the so-called girandole, which was made in small numbers between 1815 and 1818 by Lemuel Curtis. Among those who made banjo clocks were Aaron Willard, Sawin & Dyer of Boston, the New Haven Clock Company, Seth Thomas and Edward Howard.

Shelf clocks

The earlier pieces being produced at this time were usually weight-driven clocks, but by 1840 striking spring-driven clocks had been introduced. Many distinctive styles evolved during the 19th century, the best known of which is probably the shelf clock. Shelf clocks were among the earliest American clocks to be produced in any quantity and are similar in many ways to shortened longcase clocks. They are usually about 75–105 cm (2½–3½ ft) in height with an upper structure carrying the clock and dial and a base with a panel, sometimes hinged, that was finished in a variety of ways, for instance, in a wood such as mahogany, with painted decoration or with a mirror. These clocks were commonly known as 'Massachusetts shelf clocks', although they were made in several New England states. They were also known as 'box on box' or 'case on case' clocks.

Most of the movements on a shelf clock are time only, but sometimes they are equipped with an alarm and have a pendulum at the rear. There are two basic case styles. The first features the so-called kidney dial, with the name of the maker usually positioned below the chapter ring. The door frame and dial surround follow the outline of the dial. The panel in the lower part of the case is usually made of wood, with or without inlay. The other style comprises a

FAR RIGHT *Made by David Williams of Rhode Island, this shelf clock is of the kidney-dial style.*

12

round convex dial and a glazed door reverse-painted (except where the dial is). Most commonly, the panel in the box is also reverse-painted glass, but it may be mirrored or of wood.

Other distinctive styles to emerge at this time are the lighthouse clock by Simon Willard, the lyre clock, the banjo clock, the acorn clock, pillar and scroll clocks, and both steeple and steeple on steeple clocks. Novelty clocks were also popular at this time.

Torsion clocks

Another fascinating clock, which was invented in the United States but subsequently gained worldwide popularity, was the torsion clock, invented by Aaron Crane. Its escapement was activated by the very slow winding and unwinding of a steel strip. This only required minimal power and therefore made the production of one-year duration clocks a relatively easy proposition. This invention was further developed in Europe to produce the 100 day or anniversary clock.

Grandmother case clocks

Grandmother 'dwarf tall' case clocks are short longcase clocks. They were not successful, however, in part because, due to their many components, they were not much cheaper to make than a full-sized tall-case clock. Another disadvantage was that they were too short to be placed on the floor and too tall for the shelf. Most of them were made between 1810 and 1830. More grandmother case clocks by Joshua Wilder (1786–1860) have survived than by any other clock maker.

The movements of dwarf-tall clocks are often compact versions of those in tall-case clocks. However, many were just time-only, or time and alarm. Some of the cases resemble scaled-down tall-cases and have removable hoods, while others have fixed hoods with access from the rear only.

Perpetual calendar clocks

During the second half of the 19th century the perpetual calendar clock became an important item in the catalogues of Seth Thomas, E N Welch and other surviving clock companies. Seth Thomas used designs patented by his own engineers (and others), while Welch primarily used the B B Lewis patented design. The Ithaca Calendar Clock Co was formed to manufacture clocks based on H B Horton patents. Ithaca used movements made by Connecticut factories, including

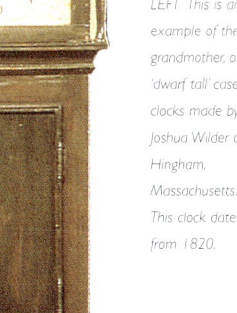

LEFT This is an example of the grandmother, or 'dwarf tall' case clocks made by Joshua Wilder of Hingham, Massachusetts. This clock dates from 1820.

WAGON SPRING CLOCK

The wagon spring clock was invented as a result of the fact that at the time there was no manufacturer of coiled springs in the United States. The wagon spring is one of the most interesting clocks of this period. Its name refers to the way in which it is driven, with a large leaf spring at the base of the clock being flexed at either end to give the clock its motive power – this resembled the spring of a wagon.

The use of a wagon spring to power a clock was pioneered by Joseph Ives of Bristol, Connecticut around 1825–30 and was continued by Birge & Fuller. Ives' clocks were of eight-day duration, but other examples made by Atkins, also of Bristol, from 1850 to 1856 went for one day or even a month. Lagville of Chalons in France made a clock powered by a wagon spring as early as 1680.

BELOW The label on the clock reads:
Patent
Accelerating Lever Spring
Eight Day Brass Clocks
Made And For Sale Wholesale And Retail By Birge & Fuller Bristol, Conn
Warranted If Well Used
Direction For Regulating The Clock
If The Clock Should Run Too Slow,
Raise The Pendulum Ball
By Means Of A Screw At The Bottom and If Too Fast Lower The Ball In The Same Manner: It Should Be Taken Off To Do It

RIGHT The line drawing of this clock explains how the mechanism works. The clock is illustrated with the left-hand train unwound. Applying the key to the winding square A the line B is drawn up and rotates the barrel C, thereby wrapping up the light chain D; this in turn draws up the lever E, which has an integral tail F. Hooked over F is a heavy link chain that connects to the outer end of the wagon spring G. This spring is firmly fixed at its centre point and, when fully wound, deflects as seen at its right-hand end in the illustration.

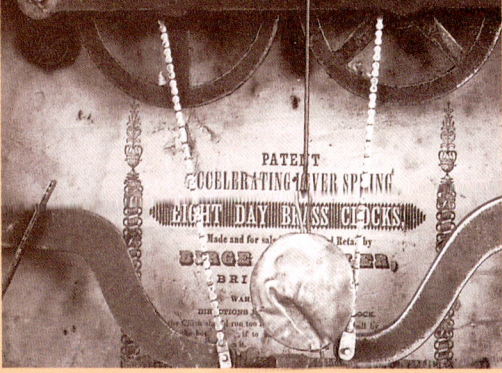

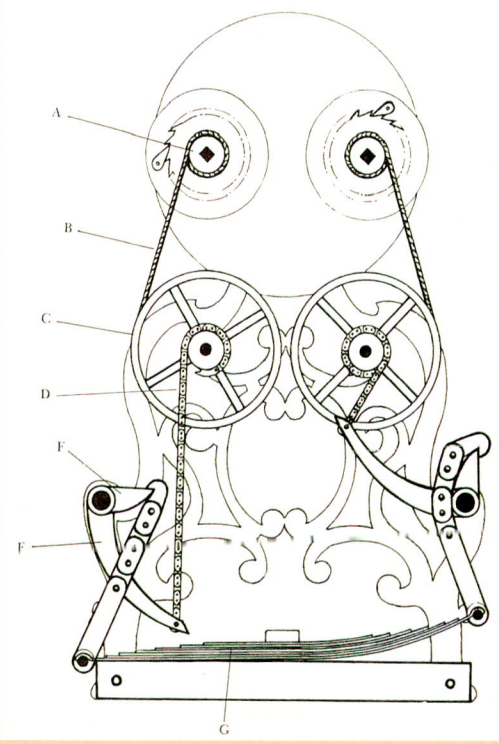

AMERICAN CLOCKS

E N Welch. It is believed that the first American calendar operated by clock machinery was patented in 1853 by an Ithaca inventor named J H Hawes, but this calendar was not 'perpetual' since it did not adjust for leap years. It was later improved by another inventor to make this adjustment and placed in the hands of James E and Eugene M Mix, also of Ithaca. The Mix brothers improved on the mechanism and obtained a patent on it in 1860, which was later purchased by the Seth Thomas Clock Company.

In 1865 H B Horton obtained a patent on an improved perpetual calendar mechanism. Later this design was further improved. Horton sold his patent to Seth Thomas of Waterbury and then went on to persuade three other Ithaca men to put up money in order to form a company to manufacture the device. With a further contribution from Horton, the new Ithaca Calendar Clock Co started business. The first clocks had iron cases and used purchased movements.

As more manufacturers began to produce shelf clocks the competition between them became increasingly fierce and various decorative features were added to improve sales. Carved designs and fancy tablets therefore became more prominent. The 'Triple-Decker' or three door shelf clock with carving and gilded columns was an attempt to incorporate all of the most desirable and expensive features in one clock.

LEFT This walnut-cased clock has two dials The upper one has minute and hour hands, the lower one is marked 1 to 31 for the days of the month.

Major manufacturers

The firm C & N Jerome only appears to have operated from 1834 to 1839. They purchased components from suppliers such as Joseph Ives and E C Brewster and Co.

LEFT Porcelain shelf clocks such as this were made during the first 20 years of this century, using American and German cases. This particular example was made by the Ansonia Clock Company – one of America's most successful clock companies.

15

AMERICAN CLOCKS

RIGHT Note how the distinctive shape of the case on this acorn clock (1835–40) is mirrored in the shape of its movement plates.

The Welch Manufacturing Company, Forestville, Connecticut, was a very successful manufacturer, and was active from c1850 until 1903, when it became The Sessions Clock Company.

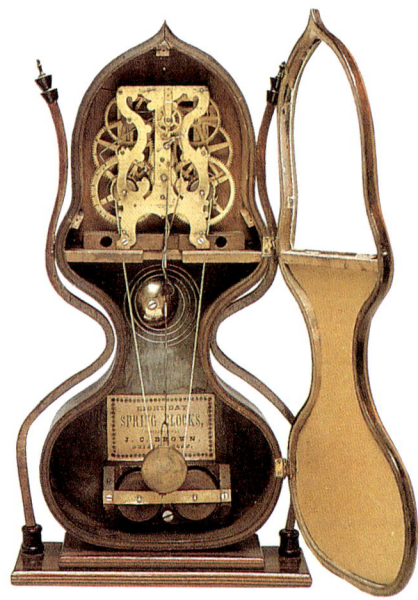

RIGHT The acorn clock, produced by J C Brown's Forestville Clock Company was unusual in its use of laminated wood, which made up the sides of the case. The glass panels on the front of these clocks were decorated with various different motifs often flowers. This example, however, shows the Merchants Exchange in Philadelphia.

William Gilbert founded his very successful clock company in 1825, and the company was to continue in business until it was sold to the Spartus Company of Chicago in 1964.

The Litchfield Manufacturing Company made 30-hour timepieces from 1851 to 1854 using movements by Matthews and Jewel of Bristol, Connecticut. In 1854 P T Barnum, a director of the firm, moved the company to East Bridgeport and joined with Theodore Terry to form the Terry & Barnum Manufacturing Company.

Iron clock cases were invented and patented by H B Horton in 1866 and produced by the J S Reynolds foundry in Ithaca for the Ithaca Calendar Clock Company in two different styles, the larger one of which is seen here. Although the cases were initially cheaper to make than wooden ones, they only stayed in production for about 10 years.

CHAPTER TWO

ENGLISH CLOCKS

• • • •

The lantern was without doubt the earliest wall clock, and first appeared in Europe, particularly southern Germany and northern Italy around 1500. Production in England, however, didn't start until some 100 years later. Lantern clocks were sometimes hung on the wall by a hoop extending backward from the top plate of the movement and engaging on a suitable hook. At the same time spikes fixed to the rear of the back feet were pushed into the wall in order to keep the clock vertical and to prevent it from moving while it was being wound. The term 'hoop and spikes' is derived from this arrangement. Alternatively, the clock was fixed to the wall by means of a bracket, usually made of oak.

The first German lantern clocks employed a verge escapement with a foliot, but this was eventually replaced by the balance wheel. All early English lantern clocks used the balance wheel.

The pendulum was discovered in 1657 and, as a result, the balance wheel became obsolete. Most of the clocks that had been made with a balance wheel were converted in order to employ the pendulum, which guaranteed far better timekeeping.

Some 12 years later the anchor escapement, usually employed with the 1 m (39 in) seconds-beating pendulum, was invented, possibly by Clement. However, the changeover from verge to anchor escapement gradually occurred in the lantern clocks over a period of 30 to 40 years. This was in part because the lantern, being a relatively simple and inexpensive clock with only an hour hand, was never expected to keep particularly good time.

BELOW Thomas Palmer of Shefford, Bedfordshire has signed the plaque on this late 17th century verge lantern clock.

17

ENGLISH CLOCKS

RIGHT Hooded wall clocks started to replace the tavern clock in the middle of the 18th century. This example was made by John Ellicott.

BELOW This late-18th-century hooded wall clock is enclosed in a mahogany case and has an engraved and silvered dial.

By the middle of the 18th century the lantern clock was going out of fashion in favour of more decorative clocks. The lantern clock was almost completely supplanted by the longcase clock, particularly the 30-hour type. Its production, however, never completely ceased in the 18th century. Another style that was to evolve – and was used by certain eminent makers such as Ellicott, John Holmes and the partnership of Thomas Mudge and William Dutton – was the hooded wall clock.

Hooded wall clocks

The hooded wall clock was produced from the late 17th to the end of the 18th century. Earlier examples usually had simple 30-hour movements with a single-handed brass dial anything from 5–10 in (13–25 cm) square. In effect they rested on a bracket and were protected by a hood that slid off this.

As the century passed, the breakarch dial came into fashion, and a minute and sometimes a seconds hand were also provided. By 1780 the painted dial was being used increasingly, but by 1800 the production of hooded wall clocks had largely ceased.

The tavern clock

By the reign of King George II a highly efficient system of coaching existed over much of Britain, making regular runs between the major cities and stopping to change horses and pick up passengers at the various coaching inns along the way. These coaches kept surprisingly accurate time, so it was essential that the inns had accurate clocks that were prominently displayed. The tavern clock fulfilled this requirement.

The tavern clock was a large weight-driven wall clock, usually enclosed within a black-lacquered case. Early examples usually have a square dial with a shallow arch at the top, following the curve of the chapter ring, and below the dial a long trunk into which the pendulum and weight extend.

Over time the dial gradually evolved from a square into a shield shape; or sometimes an octagonal shape. The circular dial probably appeared c1760 and was coloured either white or black.

By 1780–90 lacquer had started to go out of fashion for the decoration of large wall clocks such as the tavern clock. In its place mahogany was largely used. Some of the earlier examples had painted wooden dials that were left unprotected, and quite early on in the clock's history a front glass contained within a hinged brass bezel was also employed.

ENGLISH CLOCKS

The production of these clocks had largely ceased by the 1820s, although they continued to be made in Norfolk, if in a somewhat different form.

The Act of Parliament clock

Tavern clocks were also known as Act of Parliament clocks, though this name is not strictly correct, because tavern clocks were made from 1730–35 whereas the Act of Parliament that gave the clocks their name was not actually introduced until 1797.

This act imposed a duty of 5 shillings on every clock, 10 shillings on each gold watch and 2 shillings and 6 pence on those made of silver or other metals. As a result it seems that most people hid their clocks and watches to avoid paying the duty, which gave rise to a greatly increased number of large public clocks, usually tavern clocks. Inevitably the act produced a disastrous decline in the demand for watches and clocks. Clockmakers therefore petitioned Parliament and within a year the act was repealed.

Dial clocks

English cartel clocks which were similar to their French equivalent, but with cases of gilt wood rather than fire-gilt brass, started to appear c1730 and continued in production for some 50 years, though only in small numbers.

These and the circular black-dial clocks that started to be made at roughly the same time employed a spring-driven movement with a verge escapement. This form of escapement was to persist on all spring-driven wall clocks until the end of the 18th century.

Some time after the black-dial clock was produced, white-dial clocks, still employing a wooden background, came into fashion; but these were gradually replaced from the 1760s onward by the engraved and silvered brass dial, which was to remain in common use until the early 19th century. From 1780, however, the convex painted dial was to become increasingly fashionable.

LEFT The inscription at the base of this tavern clock reads Bibe, Vel Discede (Drink Up or Leave) suggesting that the clock was once used in an inn.

19

ENGLISH CLOCKS

ABOVE This late-18th-century wall clock has a silvered-brass dial signed 'Le Grave, London'. An engraved spray of flowers surrounds the city's name.

The decorative mahogany case became popular from around 1800. It was usually employed with a drop trunk that either chamfered or curved back toward the wall. Decorative brass inlay was used during the Regency period, and by c1830 there was often a glazed aperture in the front of the trunk through which the pendulum bob could be seen. By the middle of the century the convex dial had been replaced by a flat one.

The simple circular painted-dial, spring-driven fusee wall clock was produced in very large numbers throughout the entire 19th and well into the 20th century. It was used throughout England in schools, railway stations, offices and homes, and was also exported all over the world.

The weight-driven lantern clock could be difficult to accommodate because of its long pendulum and unsightly weights and rope. When reproduction lantern clocks started to be made in the mid 19th century, they therefore included a spring-driven movement and a short pendulum that was concealed within the case, so they could be placed on a table or mantelpiece. At the same time, many of the older lantern clocks were converted from weight- to spring-driven movements with a short pendulum.

A direct descendant of the cartel clock, English wall clocks with engraved and silvered-brass dials probably started to appear around 1770. They were nearly always simple timepieces, without strike, and some of the earlier examples had a cutout in the dial for the mock bob. Many had decorative engraving and beautifully executed signatures. By the early 1800s, plainer dials with simpler signatures were being produced. Examples with wooden dials were also being made; these probably continued in production for a little longer.

Around the turn of the century some particularly fine quality mahogany wall clocks were being produced; these had a trunk below the dial with what is known as a chisel base that slopes back to a sharp point at the wall. The vast majority had either painted or silvered-brass dials, but on rare occasions an enamelled dial was employed.

As the 19th century progressed painted dials became the norm. At first these were convex with a matching convex glass, but later they became flat. The standard diameter was 30.5 cm (12 in) but 25 cm (10 in) and even 20 cm (8 in) are occasionally seen.

The cases gradually became more decorative. For example inlay and carved 'ears' at either side were added. A drop was employed below the trunk, which was curved, instead of chiselled as it had been on the earlier clocks, and at a later date a brass-framed glazed aperture was provided through which the pendulum might be seen. By this time the base no longer curved back into the wall.

ENGLISH CLOCKS

LEFT Made in the late 17th century, this spring clock by John Drew, London is ebony veneered and has a square brass dial.

BELOW Although unsigned, this ebonized bracket clock is in the style typical of Ellicott.

English bracket clocks

The term bracket clock suggests that these clocks rested on a bracket, whereas in fact most of them were placed on a table, sideboard or mantelpiece. An alternative name is spring clock, however that term now could equally apply, for instance, to spring-driven wall clocks.

Bracket clocks, like longcase clocks, were first made shortly after the invention of the pendulum. However, whereas the longcase clock rapidly adopted the anchor escapement (in about 1675) with the benefit of being able to use a long seconds-beating pendulum, the anchor escapement was of far less advantage with the bracket clock. In fact it had one positive disadvantage in that it made the escapement far more critical and the clock more difficult to set up. This was of little importance with the longcase clock, but was a major factor with a bracket clock, which many would consider portable. Clocks with verge escapements are far more tolerant of being off-level and thus out of beat. It was only around 1800 that the changeover from verge to anchor escapement took place on this type of clock.

The vast majority of bracket clocks made prior to 1750 were produced in London. Even up until the turn of the century the percentage of London-made examples was relatively high. One place outside London where particularly fine clocks were made was Edinburgh.

Different styles

The design of bracket clocks has undergone a number of changes over the period of its production. These changes have related to the dial, case and components.

Earlier bracket clocks were architectural in style and ebonized. By the 1670s a few were veneered in walnut or olivewood. They bore a close resemblance to contemporary longcase clocks having brass-capped pillars at the four corners. Being so small, however, the clocks seldom featured any marquetry work.

ENGLISH CLOCKS

ABOVE A list of the 12 tunes that can be played by this musical clock are inscribed on the arch that reaches over the illustration of a parlour scene.

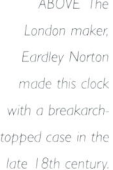

ABOVE The London maker, Eardley Norton made this clock with a breakarch-topped case in the late 18th century.

Over the period 1675–80 the architectural style started to give way to the caddy top. This was sometimes left plain and sometimes decorated with fretted and gilt-brass mounts. By 1685–90 the fretted-out gilt-brass basket top was being employed. Often this was cast, but more frequently the designs featured on it were created by *repoussé* (beaten out) work. The earliest of these were rel-

atively small and shallow, but they gradually became larger and more elaborate. Indeed, by 1710 a double-basket top was often being employed. The majority of these clocks were ebony-veneered, with only the rare model being finished in walnut, olivewood or any other similar kinds of woods.

By 1712–15 the breakarch dial was beginning to come into fashion, and in its early stages it was sometimes relatively shallow. The caddy top gradually gave way to the inverted bell, a style that was to persist well into the mid 18th century. Again the vast majority of these clocks were black, but they were usually veneered in ebonized fruitwood rather than ebony. Bracket clocks were also decorated in lacquer, but less frequently than the long-case clocks of the time. Black and red were the two colours most often used, with red being particularly popular on the later pieces. By the 1760s the inverted-bell top started to be superseded by the bell top, and other case designs evolved. It was at this stage that ebonized bracket clocks became less fashionable and mahogany took over as the favourite wood for veneering cases.

The breakarch-topped case was first produced in the 1770s, the earlier examples tending to be a little shorter and wider. The style was used both with the breakarch dial and also with a circular dial, which could either be painted or made of silvered brass. A carrying handle was employed on top; this rested on a wooden pad, often brass bound, and sometimes additional pads were placed on either side.

Up until the 1770s the brass dial incorporating a raised chapter ring and spandrels had always been employed on these clocks, but during this decade the all-over engraved and silvered brass dial started to become more and more common.

The painted or white dial also became increasingly popular from 1780 onward, but it was usually left plain with no decoration at the corners. This was probably largely because the vast majority of bracket clocks being produced at the time – and indeed throughout the last half of the 17th and the 18th centuries – originated in London. As a rule, white dials with coloured decoration were only made by companies in the country. Examples of this are the beautiful scenes that are sometimes depicted in the arch of musical bracket clocks featuring automata, such as people playing musical instruments or sawing logs.

By the 1800s painted, and occasionally silvered-brass, dials were being used almost universally on bracket clocks. The earlier dials were breakarch in form, but after this time the shape was gradually dropped in favour of the circular dial. The basic case design, however, remained the same.

LEFT Dating from c1785, this bracket clock by John Waylett has a circular painted dial, and the mahogany case if decorated with brass frets.

LEFT This Victorian triple-chain fusee bracket clock in a rosewood case has a brass dial with a raised chapter ring and cherub spandrels.

23

ENGLISH CLOCKS

RIGHT William Cribb of London made this chamfer-topped clock in c1820. The case front and chamfered corners are extensively inlaid with brass.

By the 1820s brass frets were seldom seen below the dial and clocks had become a little taller and narrower. The break at the side of the arch was now far less pronounced and was sometimes omitted. Whereas the earlier clocks had a full-width-opening front door, after c1810 just the brass bezel is hinged.

A case style that evolved at the beginning of the 19th century was the chamfer-topped bracket clock. They were usually veneered in well-figured rosewood or mahogany and sometimes inlaid with brass. In many cases a brass pineapple finial was placed on top and sometimes the top of the case was fluted.

During the Regency period several new case styles evolved. These persisted in gradually modified forms until the middle of the century and often incorporated inlaid brass. During the Victorian and Edwardian eras clocks tended to be larger and more heavily decorated, sometimes with carving, and at first the white dial predominated. However, from c1870 onward, reproductions of Georgian clocks became popular, copying their predecessors' style but sometimes being smaller and quite frequently much larger.

The 'four glass' case style also emerged during the 19th century. Featuring glass panels on all four sides, these clocks were relatively small. A height of 23 cm (9 in) was not uncommon. This style was undoubtedly stimulated by the arrival on the scene of the carriage clock and it has many similarities to that design. Sometimes these four-glass case clocks had a carrying handle on top, but more frequently this feature was omitted. Similarly, a pendulum was generally favoured and would have been provided with a clamp, although when it was likely that a particular clock would be used for frequent travelling a balance wheel escapement was employed in its place.

24

ENGLISH CLOCKS

The clocks were generally finished in handsome woods such as satinwood, mahogany, rosewood or walnut. The dials were mostly made of engraved and silvered brass but painted dials were also used, particularly on the later pieces.

Chiming

By the 1850s much larger bracket clocks were becoming popular. They were designed to provide space for a nest of bells or gongs to allow for quarter-chiming. Their introduction to the market was undoubtedly stimulated by the completion of the clock commonly known as Big Ben for the Palace of Westminster in 1859. The majority of these clocks were ebonized and embellished with ormolu mounts, but others were veneered in mahogany or rosewood.

As the century progressed, increasingly chiming was provided by a series of coiled gongs, four for Westminster – by far the most popular – and eight for other chimes, such as St Michael Gongs were also becoming more popular for the hour strike, even when bells were still used for the quarters.

The ultimate in chiming was probably the clock that was able to produce one or two different tunes on eight or sometimes even nine or ten bells. These clocks could also provide Westminster chimes on four gongs with a gong for the hour. Another Georgian influence, this time on the design, was the brass dial and sometimes an engraved backplate that appeared on most – but by no means all – of these clocks.

The end of bracket clocks

The production of most bracket clocks had virtually ceased in the United Kingdom by the early 20th century. They were largely replaced by the smaller and cheaper French and German copies of earlier English bracket clocks and by decorative French mantel clocks.

Manufacturers

Robert Halsted was an eminent clockmaker who was apprenticed to Richard Nau in 1662 and later turned over to Isaac Daniell. He became a Freeman of The

BELOW This 'four glass' clock was made in the early 19th century. As was typical of this design, there is no carrying handle on the case.

ENGLISH CLOCKS

Clockmakers Company on 6 July 1668 and within just a year he had risen to become the Master of the Company in 1699.

James Boyce of London started work in about 1685 and was a member of The Clockmakers Company. He is known to have made a silver-mounted bracket clock.

William Webster II was undoubtedly one of the finest clockmakers of the second half of the 18th century. The son of a famous father who was Thomas Tompion's journeyman, the younger Webster became a Freeman of The Clockmakers Company in 1734 and by 1755 had risen to become Master. He continued as Liveryman of the Company until 1776.

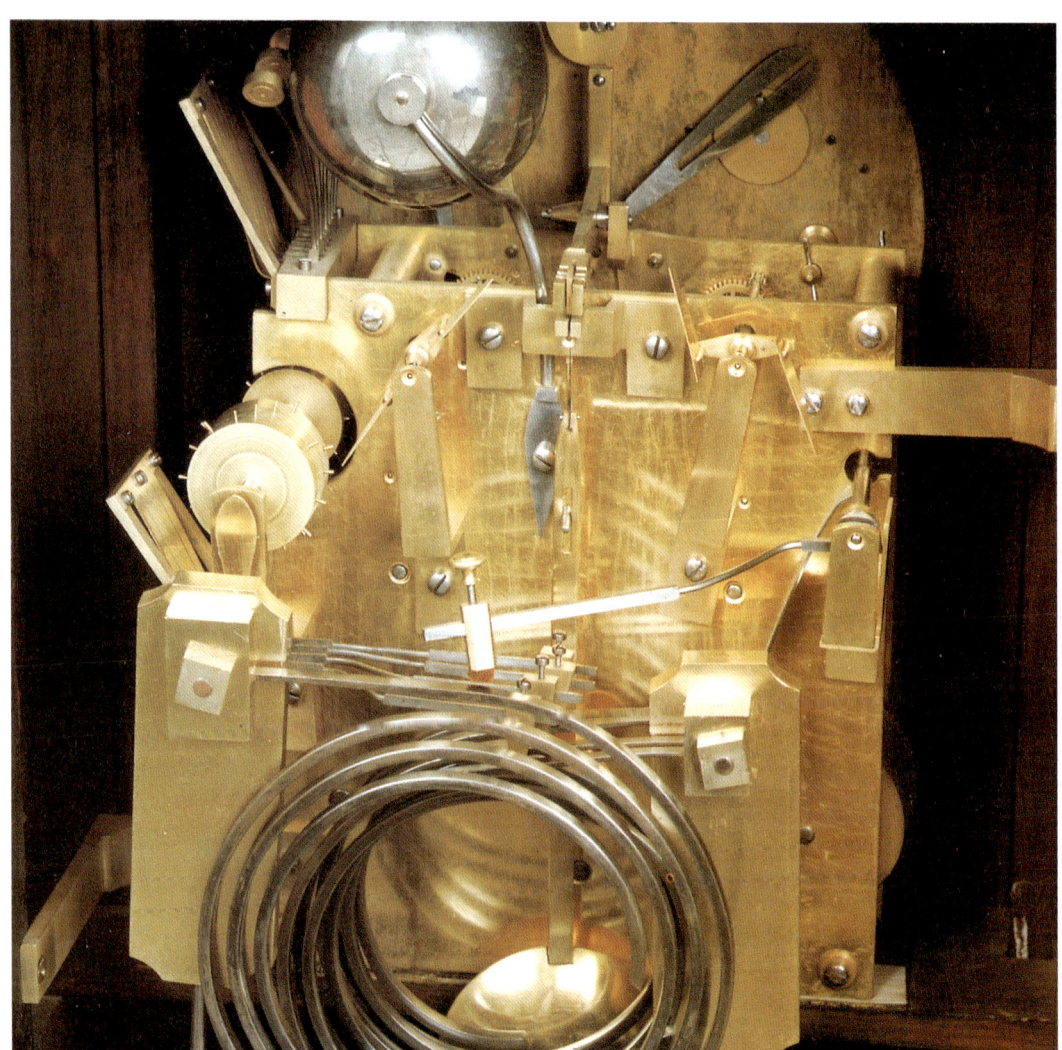

RIGHT This triple chain fusee clock has regulation for fast/slow, chime/silent and chime on Westminster chime or eight bells.

CHAPTER THREE

AUSTRO-HUNGARIAN AND DUTCH CLOCKS

• • • •

Although European countries have long been influenced by the clockmaking ideas of their neighbours, each country has developed its own style, enabling collectors to identify the origin of individual clocks.

Austro-Hungarian clocks

From 1520 to 1918 Austria was part of the Austro-Hungarian Empire, and for this reason clocks made in Austria, Hungary and

BELOW Two beautifully made, high quality 19th century Viennese wall clocks flank a German longcase clock c1880–90.

AUSTRO-HUNGARIAN AND DUTCH CLOCKS

Czechoslovakia often bear a close resemblance. Vienna, however, was the most important of the imperial courts, and consequently its influence was the strongest.

English clockmaking was very influential during the late 17th and most of the 18th century. Austrian clockmaking copied many designs and movements and even imported whole clocks. However, in 1780 it was decided to improve the standard of Austria's clock- and watchmaking by inviting some 50 Swiss craftsmen – later increased to 150 – to come and work there. Many of these were specialists and undoubtedly the skills they imparted to their Austrian colleagues provided the foundation for the beautifully executed clocks made there in the first half of the 19th century.

ABOVE This detail is taken from the top of a German musical wall clock. It was made in the Black Forest region in the first half of the 19th century. The monk seen standing in the doorway tolls the bell at each hour.

The Viennese were further influenced by the French, a bond which was reinforced by the marriage of Napoleon to Marie Louise of the House of Hapsburg in 1804. This confluence further gave rise to a renewed appreciation of classical proportions – such as those seen in the Vienna regulator. This featured a movement with exposed brass cased pendulum bob and usually weights within a fully glazed case.

However, there was a big difference between the French and Austro-Hungarian products, in that the latter were much less flamboyant and more delicately constructed than French examples. While this made them much cheaper to produce and so more affordable, it also rendered them far more appealing in many people's eyes.

RIGHT Both of these mid-19th-century wall clocks have dials with a recessed centre, commonly known as 'two-piece' dials.

28

AUSTRO-HUNGARIAN AND DUTCH CLOCKS

A golden age

The years 1800 to 1860 are considered the golden age of Austrian clockmaking. The ingenuity of the clockmakers during that period was, on many occasions, quite exceptional, with clocks being produced with various types of compensated pendulums, complex calendar work and often of long duration (up to a year and even longer). Throughout this time the number of clockmakers employed continued to increase and it was only with the onset of mass-produced clocks that the Austrian clockmaking industry began to decline.

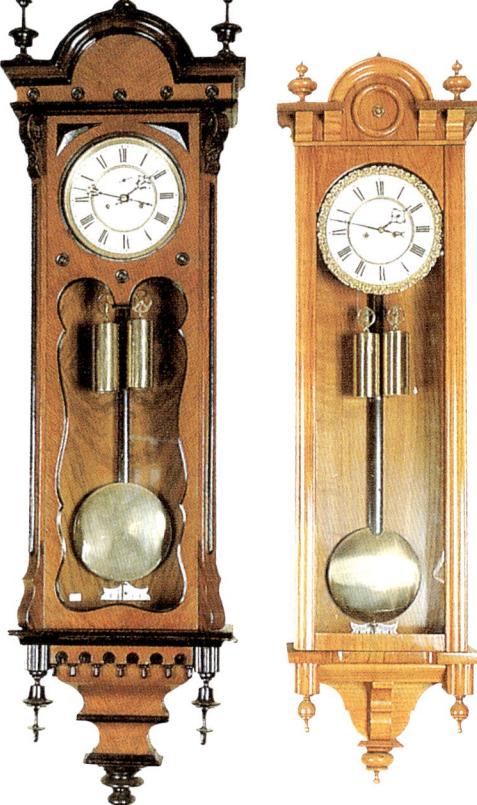

LEFT A German wall regulator (centre) with an ornate case is accompanied by two Viennese regulators that are more simple in design.

Although these later clocks were often of quite good quality, they cannot begin to compare with those that were made in the Biedermeier period in Vienna. There is only a minimum of hand-finishing, for instance. The hands were usually stamped out and the dial bezels were of simple forms and were spun up out of thin brass rather than cast.

As the end of the century approached, cases became far heavier, weighed down by what many would consider excessive ornamentation. At this time spring-driven clocks, sometimes smaller than the standard size, started to appear. No doubt this was in part to decrease the cost of manufacture, an important factor because of the intense competition from American clocks at that time.

LEFT Dating from the late 19th century, this German walnut wall regulator features a wood rod pendulum and a centre-sweep seconds hand. The movement of the clock strikes on a gong.

BELOW The two-piece dial from the satin-beech striking wall regulator (above right) has a pie-crust bezel.

AUSTRO-HUNGARIAN AND DUTCH CLOCKS

RIGHT The Hague clocks were the first pendulum clocks to be made in The Netherlands. This example is by Salomon Coster.

As a result of Christiaan Huygens, who invented the pendulum, being a regular visitor to Paris, clocks very similar to the Dutch Hague clocks appeared in the French capital at almost the same time as they began to come onto the market in The Netherlands.

These clocks soon started to lose their simplicity and gradually became more ornate as the 17th century progressed. They were either spring- or weight-driven; of single- or eight-day duration; and strike work and an alarm were often provided. Silk suspension was invariably employed for the pendulum. The dial on a Hague clock usually consisted of a velvet-covered cast-iron plate on which the silver or silvered chapter ring was mounted. This was sometimes solid and sometimes fretted out.

Dutch wall clocks

RIGHT The simple spring-driven movement of the above Hague clock has a bob pendulum and cycloidal cheeks at the top.

The first pendulum clocks to be made in The Netherlands were the so-called Hague clocks. They first appeared on the scene in the 1660s in response to the invention of the pendulum in 1657. These clocks were simple in design and rectangular in shape, and were hung from the wall by two eyelets. Early examples were usually just timepieces without any strike.

30

AUSTRO-HUNGARIAN AND DUTCH CLOCKS

The stoelklok

The Dutch *stoelklok* is basically a clock that is attached to the wall by means of a bracket. This bracket could either be very simple in design, as with the early clocks and similar to that used for lantern clocks, or it could be extremely ornate, as seen on most of the later examples that were produced during the 19th century.

The first examples of these clocks were made in or around Amsterdam, but their production rapidly spread throughout much of the country. This, of course, meant that distinct regional characteristics soon developed.

The earliest of the *stoelkloks* to be produced, which are rarely seen today, employed a balance wheel and verge escapement, but the vast majority made use of a pendulum. The earliest clocks often had a raised chapter ring set on a plain background, but within a short period the entire dial became decorated with painted scenes.

In the later period, iron or lead decoration was added to the clocks, for instance, in the form of cherubs, female figures or animals. Painted wooden figures, usually mermaids, were added to either side of the bracket at the back.

The *stoelklok* and the *staartklok* (or tail clock) dominated clock production in the Netherlands throughout the late 17th and the 18th centuries.

LEFT Made in around 1740, this stoelklok has 'ears' on either side of the back of the case. The dial and the stool on which the clock rests are both painted.

AUSTRO-HUNGARIAN AND DUTCH CLOCKS

RIGHT Mermaids and cherubs are both featured on this Dutch stoelklok. Note also the very ornate nature of the movement.

The staartklok

The *staartklok* is really a hooded wall clock and indeed it probably evolved from the earliest of these that were produced in either England or The Netherlands. The *staartklok*'s characteristic feature is the extension of the bracket down below the clock — so as, in effect, to provide a box to protect the pendulum. This box, as on the early longcase clocks, usually has a glazed aperture, which is often overlaid with decorative fretted-out gilded brass.

Early *staartkloks* tended to be fairly simple in concept and the dials were similar to those used on longcase clocks at that time. On later clocks the dial was often painted.

The clocks are normally of 30-hour duration and employ exposed brass cased weights. The majority are fairly large clocks, usually with a seconds beating pendulum, but much smaller versions were produced occasionally. Some cases were made of simple oak, but there were also variations that were ornately painted, carved and had marquetry let into them. As with the *stoelklok*, strong regional characteristics of production and design rapidly developed.

RIGHT The finials on this staartklok feature two trumpeters and Atlas carrying the world on his shoulders in the centre

CHAPTER FOUR

FRENCH AND SWISS CLOCKS

In the last half of the 17th and the 18th centuries the French approach to clockmaking was to turn out very ornate clocks to match the fashionable furniture of that time. This is scarcely surprising in a country that produced the best bronzes in the world, most of whose subjects came from mythology.

The decoration applied to the cases varied. Tortoiseshell was used extensively either on its own or in conjunction with inlaid brass (this was called Boulle work, after the inventor of the process). Silver was also let into the tortoiseshell. Horn was sometimes used as a veneer, and it was usually stained green.

In France a whole host of talent was involved: a sculptor, caster, chaser, engraver, gilder, enameller and porcelain manufacturer might all play their part in contributing to a clock's creation. The better clocks were considered to be works of art, and many fine artists were employed, for instance, to produce the patterns for the mounts applied to the case or even the whole case.

LEFT This late-18th-century French mantel clock features Astronomy reading a book, Cupid, a globe and various astronomical instruments.

33

FRENCH AND SWISS CLOCKS

RIGHT This gilt-bronze cartel clock, although signed 'London' on the dial, would in fact have been manufactured in France.

By contrast, in England the production of clocks was usually thought to require just two craftsmen, the clockmaker and the cabinetmaker.

Exotic woods such as tulipwood and kingwood, frequently laid out in geometric designs, were also used to decorate cases and increase their richness. Marquetry and parquetry were also popular methods of decorating the case.

Beautifully conceived and executed porcelain clocks were produced quite early on in the 18th century. The cases were often imported from famous factories such as Meissen and Dresden and frequently comprised flowers and figures of young girls.

Fine bronze models of animals – for instance, lions, elephants and horses – were often used, carrying the clock itself on their back, and the figure of Chronos also appeared, usually with the clock held under his arm.

French wall clocks

During the 18th and 19th centuries, the French produced two main types of wall clock, both of which they called cartel clocks. This term is used here for decorative wall clocks.

The second group is described – at least when referring to English clocks – as a bracket clock on bracket, because the two components are usually entirely separate

RIGHT A figure of the winged god Chronos (Father Time) here holds a scythe in one arm and a clock beneath the other.

34

FRENCH AND SWISS CLOCKS

from each other. In France several different terms are used for the clock bracket, such as *soubassement, console, support* or *cul de lampe*.

You may sometimes come across the word *socle* referring to the bracket, but it is possibly best to confine the use of this term to the plinth or pillar on which the clock rests.

Cartel clocks

Early in the 18th century, cartel clocks were first produced in France. They were usually made of fire gilt bronze and were beautifully chased and decorated. The first of these clocks to be made had fairly substantial movements with rectangular plates, silk suspension and verge escapements. Cartel clocks also had finely crafted convex enamelled dials and were frequently signed both on the dial and the backplate.

Cartel clocks were made until the beginning of the 19th century. Their form did change somewhat during this time, but they always tended to be fairly substantial clocks.

At the beginning of the century the mass production of French clock movements started in earnest, though the quality remained. These movements were usually smaller than their predecessors and employed circular plates, often with anchor escapements and either countwheel or rack strike. The earlier examples tended to use silk suspension.

The clocks now became, on average, much smaller in size. They remained popular throughout the 19th century, although the number produced was far less than mantel clocks, and indeed they were still being made up until the outbreak of World War 1.

LEFT The decoration on the case of this cartel timepiece shows a maiden and two winged putti amongst the shells and billowing clouds.

35

FRENCH AND SWISS CLOCKS

RIGHT Shown here on its original bracket, this musical clock by Jacquet Droz has fine ormolu mounts and a convex enamelled dial.

Bracket clock on bracket

These clocks were first produced at the beginning of the 18th century and were usually – but by no means always – large clocks anything up to 1.52 m (5 ft) in overall length. Although the clock and its accompanying bracket were two separate items, they were always conceived as one overall design, which was usually highly decorative.

The pendulum was frequently visible and the dial made up with an ornamental background on which raised enamelled numerals were placed.

Probably the most common decoration applied to the case was Boulle marquetry, that is delicate designs in brass let into a tortoiseshell background. Tortoiseshell alone, usually brown or green, was also used, in conjunction with ormolu mounts as well as lacquer decoration.

Swiss wall clocks

Pierre Jacquet Droz à La Chaux de Fonds was probably the most eminent of all Swiss clockmakers. He specialized in beautiful musical clocks, including some that even incorporated singing birds.

CHAPTER FIVE

LONGCASE CLOCKS

• • • •

The pendulum was invented in the mid 17th century and gave rise to the longcase clock. The case was originally designed as a box for protecting and hiding the relatively unsightly weights, pulleys and lines or ropes that made up the pendulum.

The pendulums used in conjunction with the verge escapement were short, averaging maybe just 23 cm (9 in) in length and having a wide arc of swing. Because the pendulum was short it could be accommodated within a narrow case, which was usually only around 1.9 m (6 ft 3 in) high. These cases, in keeping with the Puritan influence of the time, tended to be black, either making use of ebony veneers or ebonized fruitwood.

The earliest longcase clocks were generally quite small – usually less than 1.98 m (6½ ft) tall – and their simple classical proportions, based on Roman and Greek architecture, have seldom been equalled, let alone improved upon.

The first decoration to appear on the early walnut and olivewood veneered longcases was parquetry.

The anchor escapement and the 'royal' pendulum

A longer pendulum would have been impossible to confine within the case and, would have absorbed far more power. However, around 1670 the anchor escapement was invented, probably by William Clement of the UK. The difference between this and the verge which was used virtually universally until that time, is that the escape wheel is mounted parallel to all the other wheels in the clock so no contrate wheel is needed. It also requires a far narrower arc of swing and as a result, a much longer pendulum could be accommodated within a narrow case. This immediately

LEFT *Typical of early longcase clocks, this example is small and ebony veneered.*

BELOW *The latched six-pillar movement has circular cutouts at the top of the plates.*

37

LONGCASE CLOCKS

RIGHT Various parquetry designs decorate the case of this English longcase clock. Fans, circles and semi-circles accompany eight-pointed stars.

brought into being the 'royal' pendulum, which was approximately 1 m (3⅓ ft) long, and moved from side to side (beat) in exactly one second.

As a result of these new developments there were two improvements in clockmaking generally: the accuracy of clocks increased dramatically, and seconds could now be shown by a separate hand on the dial which was directly connected to the arbor (axle) on which the pallets are mounted.

Maintaining power

Following Clement's invention of the anchor escapement there were no major advances in the design of the components of a longcase clock for the next quarter of a century. However, in the 1670s, one improvement was made: 'maintaining power'. This involved an auxiliary spring that keeps the clock going while it is being wound and power is removed from the train of wheels. The first form was called 'bolt and shutter', wherein shutters covered the winding holes and could only be removed by pulling a cord or depressing a lever. This then charged a spring-loaded bolt, which pressed on a wheel in the clock and kept it going.

This form of maintaining power was not entirely successful and its use had largely been discontinued by 1700. For the same reason it has usually been removed from earlier clocks and where it is seen, it is likely to be a reinstatement. A more efficient method of maintaining power, known as 'Harrison's going ratchet', was devised a little later in the 1720s.

British longcase clocks

As the 17th century progressed longcase clocks gradually increased in height, probably averaging 2.1 m (7 ft) without a caddy and 2.26 m (7 ft 5 in) with one by around 1700. At the same time the dials, which were always square, became larger, being 25.4 cm (10 in) or less in the early days, then 28 cm (11 in) and finally 30.5 cm (12 in). This larger size remained by far the most popular for the rest of the life of the longcase clock.

An arch was added to the top of the square dial around 1710–15. This major change gave additional space on which to place various features such as a name plaque, strike/silent regulation or calendar work. Although at least 95 per cent of the

LONGCASE CLOCKS

ABOVE The square dial of this William Speakman clock (shown left) has the largest form of cherub spandrels, a narrow seconds ring with a cutout for the central alarm disc and a date aperture above 6 o'clock.

clocks made in London after this time employed the breakarch, the square dial remained fashionable, particularly in the country, and continued to be used well into the 19th century.

Case styles varied throughout the country and over time. Once ebony had gone out of fashion, walnut became the most popular wood for veneering clock cases in London. In the country, however, oak had always been popular and continued to be used. When walnut was the chosen wood, it could be either highly figured or relatively plain.

Marquetry

By the 1670s, as the austere influence of the Puritans declined, ebonized cases started to give way to cases veneered in woods such as walnut and olivewood. It was not long before these were decorated, first with parquetry, which is formed from geometric designs let into the case, and subsequently marquetry, which was usually floral in design and often included birds.

Originally marquetry was confined to panels laid on the trunk door and base, but later it spread to involve the hood and gradually most of the case. Toward the end of the 17th century floral marquetry started to give way to arabesques, comprising bold contrasting strapwork, usually in a dark wood laid on a light background and frequently incorporating figures, butterflies and birds. 'Seaweed', which consists of a delicate tracery made up of just two different woods was the final development in marquetry designs.

Inevitably there was overlap of marquetry styles, and it was by no means unusual to see floral marquetry in use as late as 1710. It even staged a brief

BELOW The door of this English longcase clock is inlaid with panels of floral marquetry.

BELOW LEFT At first marquetry was only used on the trunk and base of clocks.

LONGCASE CLOCKS

revival in the Victorian and Edwardian eras. However, at roughly the same time that the breakarch style was coming into favour, the use of marquetry went out of fashion.

Chinoiserie

Chinoiserie or lacquer work is the decoration of furniture and other objects with gilded gesso (a form of plasterwork), which is laid on a japanned or hard coloured lacquered background. It has been used in the Far East for at least 2,000 years, but it only appeared in Europe following increased trade with the Orient in the 15th century, first in Venice and Genoa, then Portugal and, finally, The Netherlands and England some 200 years later. In the early 1600s probably only small pieces such as tea caddies were imported, but later larger items such as wall panels were shipped back. However, it was very rare for large pieces of furniture to be imported and the number of pieces sent out to the Far East for decoration was very small.

In the first part of the 18th century, the leading English clockmakers were vying with each other to make the finest and most complex clocks, sometimes of long

LEFT Signed by the ingenious clockmaker Daniel Delander, this clock was made in London in about 1715.

duration, maybe quarter-chiming or musical, and occasionally incorporating astronomical features.

Lacquer decoration was first used on furniture in The Netherlands c1660 and somewhat later in England. However, it was probably never used on clock cases prior to 1690. Although lacquer clocks were made in England at the end of the 17th century, it was not until around 1720 that they were produced in any numbers. Lacquering never completely went out of fashion and it staged a recovery under the influence of cabinetmakers such as Chippendale in the third quarter of the 18th century.

Black was probably the most common colour used, but red, tortoiseshell and green were also employed. White is rarely seen on any of these clocks.

LEFT An early example of an English lacquer longcase clock by Henry Fish.

LONGCASE CLOCKS

Mahogany

Walnut furniture started to become less popular in Britain in the 1720s. This was for a number of reasons, one of them being the decreasing supply, caused by the loss through disease of many trees, particularly in France. The situation became so serious that export from France was banned.

Another strong influence was the increasing import of mahogany from the West Indies and America following England's rapidly growing trade in those areas. The timber that the English imported, mainly from Cuba and Honduras, was ideal for cabinetmaking: it was not subject to attack by worm (as was walnut), it was available in long, wide boards and it could also be obtained highly figured, such natural patterning being ideal for veneers.

The earlier mahogany clock cases tended to be fairly plain, but by 1765–85 cases of the very highest quality with superb veneers were being produced. However, by the end of the century only a small number of longcase clocks were still being produced in London, and those made in the Regency period tended to have circular dials, either painted or of silvered brass.

The classic London mahogany pagoda-topped clock gradually evolved over a period of 40 to 50 years. It was initially developed from the caddy top.

These clocks often had brass stringing added to the hood columns, and brass-capped quarter columns were frequently applied to either side of the trunk. The wooden fret employed in the pagoda to let the sound out was sometimes replaced by a decorative brass fret. The cases produced in London at that time were among the finest ever made.

Country mahogany longcase clocks

Longcase clocks from the provinces of England showed far more individuality and, some would say, character than those made in London. They frequently developed regional characteristics and their quality, especially in the last half of the 18th century, was often excellent. In the seafaring West Country the clocks frequently featured rolling moon discs in the arch with ships and often showed the time of high water at a particular port. A wavy border was sometimes a part of the inner aspect of the hood door and rope-twist columns were also popular decorative devices.

LEFT This pagoda-topped longcase clock by John Monkhouse is typical of the high quality of work in London towards the end of the 18th century.

LONGCASE CLOCKS

ABOVE *The dial of this English longcase clock has a beautifully engraved centre and the phases of the moon are shown in the arch of the dial.*

In more remote areas entirely different designs evolved: for instance, the swan-neck pediment, immensely popular in the country, was scarcely ever seen on London-made clocks.

Thirty-hour clocks

A '30 hour' clock is one that will run for a little more than a day. This gives the flexibility of being able to wind the clock a few hours later than usual without it stopping. Very few of these were made in London but they were particularly popular in the country districts because they were small and therefore relatively affordable.

Up until around 1770 30-hour clocks usually had solid oak cases and a square brass dial, frequently 25.4 cm (10 in), but on the later clocks 28 cm (11 in) or 30.5 cm (12 in) square. The early clocks only had a single hand (no minute hand) and virtually all 30-hour clocks are driven by a single weight that is rewound every day by pulling down on a rope or chain. This means that the clock continues to keep time while being wound, and no winding holes are required in the dial.

From the early 1700s onward, simple longcase clocks of only 30-hour duration started to be made for farmworkers' cottages. These were usually less than 1.98 m (6½ ft) tall to suit the low ceilings and the earlier clocks generally had a 24.5 cm (10 in) square brass dial with just a single (hour) hand that was quite accurate enough for the owners' lifestyles. As the century progressed the addition of the minute

RIGHT *Produced in Lancashire, England, this longcase clock demonstrates the character and quality of clocks from outside London.*

42

LONGCASE CLOCKS

hand became common, and the dial became somewhat larger, either 28 cm (11 in) or 30.5 cm (12 in). By 1780–90 the painted dial had largely replaced the brass dial and more decorative cases, often veneered in mahogany, were produced. However, by then the manufacture of 30-hour clocks was rapidly declining in favour of those that had an eight-day duration.

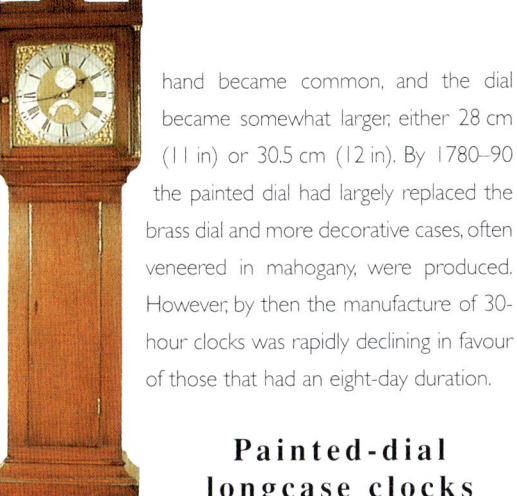

Painted-dial longcase clocks

The white-painted dial longcase clock started to appear in the 1770s and, although very few were made in London, they rapidly replaced the brass dial elsewhere in the country. They had a number of advantages, in that they were easier to read, cheaper to produce and many would say far more decorative. Before the century was out the painted-dial clocks were probably outselling those with brass dials by at least ten to one.

The first recorded reference to white dials, unearthed by Brian Loomes, appeared in the *Birmingham Gazette* in 1772. It read as follows:

'Osborne and Wilson, manufacturers of white clock dials in imitation of enamel, in a manner entirely new, have opened a warehouse at No 3 in Colmore Row, Birmingham. Where they have an assortment of the above mentioned goods. Those who favour them with orders may depend upon their being executed with the utmost punctuality and expedition.'

The earliest white dials sometimes had no decoration other than the numerals and the signature, or just spandrels in the form of raised gilt decoration in the four corners. However, they soon became more colourful, typically displaying flowers such as roses and peonies in the corners and, if

LEFT *Made with the low ceilings of farmworkers' cottages in mind, clocks such as this example were usually less than 1.9 m (6½ ft) tall.*

RIGHT *The arch of this longcase clock shows the moon phases, while the girls in the corners of the dial depict the four seasons.*

LONGCASE CLOCKS

ABOVE *The star studded disk in the arch of this clock displays the various phases of the moon.*

there was no moon disc, also in the arch. If there was a moon disc and the clock was made near the coast, particularly in the West Country, then ships were featured, but inland buildings were often chosen, at least in part, as the subject. Another popular feature was to illustrate the four seasons by means of flowers, crops or girls dressed in suitable costumes or carrying out activities associated with the different times of the year. As the 19th century progressed, the decoration on the dial increased further. The corners were filled in solid and the arch often showed various scenes and people. By the 1850s, shortly before the demise of the longcase clock, virtually the whole of the dial was covered with decoration.

Complex clocks

In the period 1720–80 a considerable number of complex clocks were made in Britain. Some of these would chime the quarters, usually on eight bells, and others would play a tune either every one or three hours or at will. Other clocks provided complex astronomical information.

Some of these clocks were even designed to go for longer than one week. A month was the period most often chosen and this was particularly popular from 1670 to 1710, but clocks of three, six and even 12 months running were also made.

RIGHT *Charles Clay of London produced this quarter-chiming longcase clock. Note how the breakarch top is repeated in the trunk door.*

LONGCASE CLOCKS

French longcase clocks

France produced hardly any longcase clocks, in the English sense of the term, but they did make clocks that resembled English models in some ways. In the 18th century, for example, the French sometimes placed their clocks on decorative matching pillars, which in effect gave them a similar height and width to a longcase clock. Also, from 1760 onward they housed their regulators in far more restrained one-piece cases of superb quality, which by 1780–1810 were often free of all ornamentation.

In the country districts of France in the 19th century considerable numbers of what might be termed longcases were made in order to house what were known as Comtoise clocks (from the clockmaking district, Franche-Comté). These usually had ornamental, thin-pressed brass dials with enamelled centres and frequently very large and decorative pendulums, although on the earlier clocks these tended to be plain. The cases were usually made of local woods such as apple, cherry or pine. These clocks struck at the hour and then repeated it again at two minutes past.

American longcase clocks

The first settlers in the New World would have brought the earliest clocks to America. These would probably have been relatively small clocks such as lanterns, not longcase clocks, which would have been expensive to transport. Among these early settlers were an ever increasing number of blacksmiths and clockmakers. Abel Cottey (d 1717) from Crediton in Devon was one of the first recorded craftsmen, having emigrated in 1682 to Philadelphia, where he is known to have prospered and made longcase clocks.

LEFT This English astronomical longcase clock by Edward Cockey, shows the superb craftsmanship of early 18th century country clockmakers.

LEFT The dish within the 24-hour chapter ring is painted to represent the day and night skies. A cast gilt figure of Father Time indicates the hour.

45

LONGCASE CLOCKS

RIGHT This American tall clock by Isaac Brokaw of New Jersey has brass instead of wood winding-drums and brass instead of steel pillars.

By the early 18th century clockmaking was fairly well established in New York, New England, Pennsylvania and Virginia, and was conducted in much the same way as it was back in England at that time. As the 18th century progressed, clockmaking gradually spread over a much wider area, although it flourished in certain places, such as Connecticut.

The basic methods of clock construction in the American colonies were similar to those used in England, but they had to be adapted to the materials available in the area. Brass, for instance, was in short supply, so makers would sometimes use wood as a substitute, or use the metal in strip form. Similarly, local woods such as cherry were employed for the case.

Some complete longcase clocks were imported, but it was more usual to bring just the movements (complete with dials) and then to manufacture the cases locally. Many components were also imported. This sometimes meant whole movements and dials, but in other instances just wheels, pinions, barrels, plates, hands, pendulum bobs and so on were brought over.

Prior to the War of Independence it is likely that only a fairly small but gradually increasing number of longcase – or tall-case as they are referred to in the United States – clocks were produced. By the early 19th century the first examples of smaller mass-produced clocks were starting to make an appearance on the market.

American clockmakers

The Willards of Massachusetts evolved their own style of case and movement in the guise of the banjo clock, and Gideon Roberts in Bristol, Connecticut, produced wall clocks with wooden movements.

The Willards were one of the most important families in the history of clockmaking in the United States. They started their business with the manufacture of traditional English handcrafted clocks and continued to be successful right through into the era of volume production.

Aaron Willard (1757–1844) made more clocks than his brothers, but Simon (1753–1848) was the innovator. It was he who made the banjo wall clock – the first successful, truly American design.

46

LONGCASE CLOCKS

Isaac Brokaw was apprenticed to Aaron Miller. He completed his apprenticeship and married Miller's daughter in 1766, and continued in business until 1816.

In 1773 Thomas Harland emigrated from England to settle in Norwich, Connecticut, where he continued to make clocks in the traditional English way. He passed these methods on to his apprentices, one of whom was Daniel Burnap, who in turn had Eli Terry as an apprentice.

Harland's clocks were usually housed in rather plain cases with frets at the top of the hood that are referred to as 'whale's tails'; hence the name whale's tail (or Norwich) case.

Eli Terry (1772–1853) was born in East Windsor, Connecticut, the son of Samuel and Hildah Burnham Terry. He was apprenticed to Daniel Burnap of East Windsor, and had started work on his own account by 1792. He made tools for the manufacture of wooden clocks in quantity using water-powered saws, and in 1797 he patented a clock showing mean and solar time, the first of his many inventions (another was a machine for cutting gear wheels). Among his many achievements was the design of a movement for a wall clock that would run for 30 hours on a 51 cm (20 in) fall of the weight. This was a development that made the production of shelf clocks, which were considerably cheaper than longcase clocks, possible.

The Porter contract

Eli Terry entered into what was probably the most significant contract in manufacturing history in 1806, when he undertook a commission to deliver 4,000 30-hour wooden movements, dials, hands, pendulums and weights to Levi and Edward Porter of Waterbury.

Subsequently known as the 'Porter Contract', the order was completed by 1810. It was, of course, only made possible by the complete interchangeability of all the components. This was something that had not been attempted before and it could be said to signal the birth of mass production.

LEFT This American tall-case clock with a pine case of New England styling contains an Eli Terry wooden movement as shown below.

LEFT An Eli Terry movement of 30-hour duration. These were made as part of the Porter Contract to supply 4,000 movements, dials, hands, pendulums and weights.

47

LONGCASE CLOCKS

RIGHT Made by Jan van der Swelling in c1770, this longcase clock has typical Dutch finials: two angels and the figure of Atlas carrying the world.

Eli Terry's contract subsequently gave rise to some 200 manufacturers in western Connecticut making hundreds of thousands of clocks annually, all using similar wooden movements to those devised by Terry. This continued until the 1830s, when the ready availability of rolled brass meant that it replaced wood.

Dutch longcase clocks

Longcase clocks were first produced in The Netherlands fairly shortly after the invention of the pendulum. These early clocks usually had a walnut case of simple, but pleasing proportions resting on bun feet and were 2.1 m (7 ft) or less in height. They employed spiral twist columns to the hood and were usually surmounted by carved decoration that was frequently quite elaborate.

The square dial of these clocks often had an iron, velvet-covered plate onto which the raised chapter ring and spandrels were applied. Ornamental gilt-brass hands were used in order to contrast with the black velvet. By the end of the first quarter of the 18th century the arched dial had been adopted, often displaying the moon phases. The clocks had also become much taller and frequently employed a *bombé* base.

Dutch striking, in which the clock strikes out the hours in full both at the halves on a high bell and at the hour on a lower tuned bell, usually featured in these longcase designs, and an alarm was frequently incorporated. A number of musical clocks were also made. They were usually tall and often quite complex clocks, for instance, with large apertures in the centre of the dial for the days of the week and the months of the year, which were represented by paintings or engravings of the deities and the zodiacal signs.

Many of the most elaborate clocks, anything up to 3–3.35 m (10–11 ft) tall, had a mounting on the top of the case of one or more figures, the most common being Atlas supporting the world.

In The Netherlands during the 18th century the number of longcase clocks to be produced gradually declined, while the demand for wall clocks increased. By contrast, in England, the production of longcase clocks rapidly increased over the same period of time.

CHAPTER SIX

CARRIAGE CLOCKS

F ollowing the invention c1500 of the coiled spring to power clocks, the travelling clock became a far more practical proposition. Although portable weight-driven clocks were made, these were difficult to use, because a special box was required to keep the clock and weights together: each time it was moved, it had to be packed up and reset in its new location by hanging it on the wall and adding the weights. A spring-driven clock had none of these problems.

Probably the earliest travelling clocks, if we ignore the watch, which is only for personal use, were those made in southern Germany, such as the rectangular or hexagonal table clocks, which often originally had travelling cases. Similar clocks were also made in both France and Italy.

The coach watch was another form of travelling clock, and was in fact very similar to a giant watch. In England small bracket clocks were made with travelling cases.

French carriage clocks

The major developments in travelling clocks took place in France. Apart from the clock termed *pendule de voyage*, two distinct styles evolved, one the *pendule d'officier*, the other the *Capucine*. Neither of these, however, had a particularly long life, and soon disappeared with the advent of the carriage clock.

ABOVE A later example of a French carriage clock by Paul Garnier, dated 1845.
LEFT Designed by Abraham Louis Breguet, this clock is seen with its carrying box, key and certificate.

49

Manufacturers

The first carriage clocks were made by Abraham Louis Breguet, but only in very small numbers for they were both very expensive and usually complex. Although the basic design of these clocks was conceived during Breguet's lifetime, they went on to be produced long after his death. In fact, many of the later pieces that were made in the last part of the 19th century and the beginning of the 20th century were 'bought in' pieces. These were not made by Breguet, but were retailed having had the name added.

Paul Garnier (1801–69) was the first to produce carriage clocks in any quantity and usually employed his own form of escapement, the chaffcutter. By the late 1830s he had been joined by other makers such as Bolviller, Auguste, Jules, Berolla and Lépine, and by the 1850s carriage clock production was in full swing, with all the benefits that mass production can bring. Blondeau was another well-known early French maker, examples of whose work are rare. He exhibited in Paris in 1827, 1834 and 1837.

As the century went on, the market tended to expand. Some of the best-known makers were: Drocourt, Couaillet, Dumas, Duverdrey & Bloquel, Jacot, Japy Frères, Lamaille, Henry Marc, Margaine, Maurice, Pons, Richard & Cie and Soldano. However, it is difficult to know in what quantities the clocks were made, as the majority are unsigned. Most retailers preferred to have just their own name on the dial.

Different styles

Many different case styles evolved and sizes also varied enormously. Although the majority were between 11.4 cm (4½ in) and 16.5 cm (6½ in) high, excluding the handle, miniatures of only a little over 5 cm (2 in) were produced, as well as giants going up to 25.4 cm (10 in).

RIGHT A French carriage clock decorated with multicoloured champlevé enamelling.

CARRIAGE CLOCKS

another. Decorative porcelain panels, often on a romantic theme were also used to substitute the glass panels and plain white dials.

Another popular form of ornamentation was multi-coloured *champlevé* enamelling, a process in which lacunae (recesses) are cut in brass and then filled with different colours of enamel that are fired individually in a furnace at relatively high temperatures. Enamelled panels, usually Limoges, were also used, as were those

The gorge case, with its attractive moulds and fluting at the front four corners, was one of the finest and certainly the most popular case style to evolve c1860.

By about 1860 it became fashionable to decorate carriage clocks with fine panels, often incorporating semi-precious stones. However, these were only ever produced in relatively small numbers as they were expensive to make.

Engraving was one of the most common types of decoration that was introduced in order to make the carriage clock more appealing. The quality and extent of the engraving varied greatly from one manufacturer to

LEFT Dating from c1835, this is a relatively early French carriage clock. It is shown with its original carrying case, which is also early in style.

LEFT The beautiful Sèvres porcelain panels on this French, gorge-cased clock are all decorated with beads of semiprecious stones and pearls.

51

CARRIAGE CLOCKS

RIGHT Dating from c1850, this English carriage clock is superbly cast, chased and engraved. It has highly decorative columns and side panels.

decorated with multicoloured gold and silver. One of the most beautiful finishes to be applied to a carriage clock was that of combined multicoloured golds and silver, which were let into the metal of the case, usually against a dark background. Not surprisingly, this was a particularly expensive and time-consuming technique.

Carriage clock production continued at a relatively high level up until the outbreak of the First World War in 1914. Although production did start again after 1918, far fewer clocks were produced and their output continued to decrease steadily until by 1939 it was very small indeed. Carriage clocks have never entirely lost their appeal however and have continued to be made. Probably more carriage clocks are being produced today than in the past 30 to 40 years – proof of their enduring popularity.

RIGHT An engraved mask surrounds the circular silvered dial. The clock contains an English timepiece movement.

52

CARRIAGE CLOCKS

usually far larger, heavier and much more expensive to manufacture; many still employed chain fusees. The English did produce a few small carriage clocks that were generally simple timepieces, often without a fusee. Quite contrary to the French approach, most English clocks were made with an apparent disregard for expense and the incorporation of such features as a chronometer escapement.

Travelling cases tended to be made of wood, rather than the leather of the French clocks. Whereas in France there were a relatively large number of carriage clock manufacturers, in England production was confined to a few of the top names, such as McCabe, Frodsham, Dent, Vulliamy, Barwise, Smith and Jump.

In an attempt to produce a viable alternative to the French carriage clock, a few small English carriage timepieces with a going barrel (no fusee) and without strike were made, which usually had solid sides and a back door. They do not appear to have been a success, however.

LEFT Signed by well known makers, S Smith and Sons of London, this carriage clock shows one of the most popular case styles.

BELOW A Swiss pendule d'officier made in Geneva by Robert & Courvoisier.

English carriage clocks

Although carriage clocks started to be made in England at roughly the same time as they did in France, no serious attempt was made to compete with the French carriage clock industry. The clocks made in England were

Swiss carriage clocks

The Swiss produced a limited number of carriage clocks similar to those made in the

53

CARRIAGE CLOCKS

RIGHT This Austrian carriage clock by Michael Gruebmüllner shows a painted dial with flowers at the corners and a landscape in the arch.

ture Swiss carriage clocks was produced around Geneva by firms such as the Geneva Clock Company. These were usually beautifully decorated with coloured enamels, and the best of them were retailed by firms such as Cartier and Asprey.

Austrian carriage clocks

During the first half of the 19th century the Viennese produced a most attractive series of distinctive Austrian travelling or carriage clocks that were entirely different from the French models. They were nearly always of only two-day duration, had grande-sonnerie striking, usually with an alarm, and often employed a duplex escapement. Quite often the cases were heavily engraved and fire gilt.

American carriage clocks

Carriage clocks were mass-produced by just a few American firms. These pieces were usually of relatively simple design, sometimes copying those clocks produced in France and in other instances evolving their own distinctive American styles.

Franche-Comté region of France in the earlier period. Two of the most famous makers were the Courvoisiers, Frédéric and Auguste. It is likely that the majority of the later carriage clocks bearing Swiss names were made either in whole or in part in France. However, from around 1900 to 1930, a most attractive range of minia-

The Waterbury Clock Company undoubtedly made a large number of carriage clocks, but they were also produced by the Ansonia Clock Company, Chauncey Jerome, Seth Thomas, the Boston Clock Company and the Vermont Clock Company.

CHAPTER SEVEN

SKELETON CLOCKS

● ● ● ●

The skill and ingenuity of the clockmaker were the main features in the design of the skeleton clock. No case was provided, just a protective glass dome or a glazed brass frame through which the clock could be seen. The dial was frequently fretted out and its centre omitted; the movement plates, particularly on English clocks, were also fretted out.

French skeleton clocks

During the last half of the 18th century this design of clock gradually evolved from the fine *pendules de cheminée* being made in France.

It was a time of patronage and also great wealth, albeit for a relatively small number of people. Customers demanded and wanted to be seen to have the best and, happily, this coincided with the greatest period in French clockmaking with such superb makers as Janvier, Berthoud, Lépine, the Lepautes, Bailly and Breguet, to name but a few.

Up until around 1800 French skeleton clocks all tended to be different, and they were often very complex, employing for instance, a *remontoir* most commonly a device for converting a spring-driven clock into a weight-driven one by using the mainspring to wind up a small weight at regular, generally short, intervals. This device provides much more even power than a spring and thus improves the timekeeping of the piece.

LEFT The movement on this Viennese clock is seen through the chapter ring.

55

SKELETON CLOCKS

RIGHT A French Great Exhibition skeleton clock designed by Victor Pierret.

Other additional features added to the clock at this time included the moon's age and phases, simple and perpetual calendar work, and an additional hand. This means that both mean time and solar time are shown on these clocks and thus also the 'equation of time', that is the difference between mean time and that shown on a sundial.

The French glass-plated skeleton clocks, which were first made around the beginning of the 19th century, are without doubt the ultimate in the design of skeleton clocks. All of their wheelwork appears to be suspended in midair, as there is no visible frame. The execution of these clocks is always a joy to behold.

ABOVE The delicate wheelwork on this French glass plated clock is seen through a glass plate that is supported on two gilded scrolls resting on a white marble base. Note the enamelled chapter ring with decorated numerals.

SKELETON CLOCKS

(10 in) tall. Victor Pierret of Paris designed the clock and went on to produce it from the 1840s until the end of the century.

This particular design of clock appeared in a variety of forms. For instance, it was available with and without engraving and it might have an alarm concealed within the base and wound by a cord coming out of one side. A second cord on the other side was provided to set the time at which the alarm went off by rotating the alarm disc in the centre of the dial.

Following their appearance at the Great Exhibition, where they sold in relatively large numbers, these clocks were commonly known as Great Exhibition skeleton clocks. They then went on to be produced over a long period and in appreciable numbers.

LEFT Topped by a lunar dial, this French clock shows strong Egyptian and Roman influence.

BELOW This Austrian clock is decorated with gold leaf and silver repoussé work.

After 1800–10, although fascinating one-off clocks continued to be produced, a small number of certain standardized designs were made. Examples of these are the beautiful glass-plated clocks, possibly the ultimate in skeleton-clock design, which can go for six months on one winding. A similar but keyhole-framed design was also produced, and Verneuil made a series of fine and often quite large calendar skeleton clocks.

One of the best known French skeleton clocks was that shown at the Great Exhibition in London in 1851. This small but attractive piece was only around 25.4 cm

Austrian skeleton clocks

The manufacture of skeleton clocks in the Austro-Hungarian Empire was mainly concentrated in Vienna and commenced around the beginning of the 19th century. Although initially these Austrian models were quite often strongly influenced by similar clocks made in France, they soon

57

SKELETON CLOCKS

went on to assume a character all of their own. Many of the earlier examples of these clocks were of considerable complexity and ingenuity – for instance, quite a few of them were weight-driven. The later pieces, however, were more standardized. They were usually spring-driven, of two-day duration and had quarter-striking. Later examples were also far more ornate in their design.

RIGHT This selection of skeleton clocks all dating from the mid 19th century, shows the variety of forms that this design can take.

SKELETON CLOCKS

English skeleton clocks

In England the manufacture of skeleton clocks commenced around 1820. Earlier pieces tended to copy the more basic French styles and would usually have an inverted Y-shaped frame. Relatively few skeleton clocks were made prior to 1835, but after this time production escalated rapidly, no doubt strongly influenced by the increasing momentum of the Industrial Revolution. Indeed, by 1850–60 the numbers being made vastly exceeded those that had been produced in France and Austria.

The Gothic frame

One of the first of what might be called the purely English designs was the simple Gothic frame – which followed close on the heel of the inverted Y-frame.

The Gothic frame was usually only 28–30.5 cm (11–12 in) tall and was generally just a timepiece. This design reached its peak of popularity between

FAR LEFT This English skeleton clock plays music from a selection of six tunes every two hours. It is, however, silent at night and on Sundays.

LEFT This c1840 example of an English Gothic-frame clock has stepped frames surmounted by crosses.

59

1835 and 1850, after which time it tended to be replaced by the architectural clocks. The Gothic frame was quickly followed by the scroll frame, which was first produced by Edwards of Stourbridge.

RIGHT An English skeleton clock on a carved mahogany base produced c1840 by James Condliff, one of the finest skeleton clock makers.

At this time the range of clocks available increased rapidly. Even musical clocks were now being produced, and the variety of frames was greatly extended. By around 1845 skeleton clocks based on famous buildings started to appear. One of the first buildings to be copied was the Scott Memorial, which had recently been completed in Edinburgh. This clock was produced by Evans of Handsworth (Birmingham) and sold in large numbers throughout Scotland.

Other buildings copied included York Minster, Westminster Abbey, Lichfield Cathedral and the Brighton Pavilion. Floral designs were also produced, incorporating, for instance, fuchsias and ivy leaves.

Manufacturers

The vast majority of skeleton clocks in England were produced by a few specialist manufacturers, such as Evans of Handsworth (Birmingham) and Smith of Clerkenwell (London). There were however other clockmakers of the time who, although they made relatively small numbers of skeleton clocks, produced some highly ingenious pieces of superb quality. For example, James Condliff made some beautifully proportioned and excellently crafted clocks, which quite frequently employed a seconds-beating balance. Pace also produced some fascinating clocks at this time.

By 1890 the heyday of the English skeleton clock was over and 20 years later only a few simple timepieces were being produced.

CHAPTER EIGHT

MYSTERY, NOVELTY AND FANTASY CLOCKS

Some clocks are designed not just to tell the time, but to fascinate in one way or another. They may mystify you as to how they work or amuse you with the way in which they do so. These designs often used automata (moving figures) that perform either while the clock is ticking or just when it strikes.

The first in this line of clocks originated in the 17th century in southern Germany. Pieces were produced in the forms of animals and people whose eyes moved in time with the pendulum. Others were far more complex, for example, the arms, legs, neck or head might move, imitating an action such as eating. One of the most fascinating is the Chariot Clock, which can be seen in The Time Museum, Rockford, Illinois. This clock shows the gluttonous mythical King Gambrinus sitting on a chariot, which can move down the dining table under its own power. As the clock moves, the monarch raises a tankard in his right hand to his mouth, which opens and closes as he does so.

In the 19th century the French produced a series of clocks designed to mystify everyone regarding how they worked. These clocks have no apparent movement behind the dial, for example, or the hands, mounted on a glass dial, appear to have no possible means of driving them,

ABOVE A French mystery clock dating from about 1870.

LEFT The John Bull blinking-eye clock by Bradley and Hubbard, Connecticut.

MYSTERY, NOVELTY AND FANTASY CLOCKS

FAR RIGHT An American swinging clock made by the Ansonia Clock Company in c1890. The figure of a girl holds the double-sphere pendulum.

RIGHT The arms of a young girl indicate the time on this rare French mystery clock. Her right hand points to the hours, her left to the minutes.

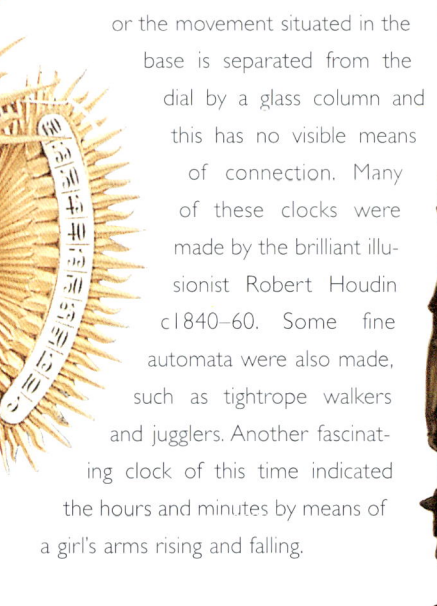

or the movement situated in the base is separated from the dial by a glass column and this has no visible means of connection. Many of these clocks were made by the brilliant illusionist Robert Houdin c1840–60. Some fine automata were also made, such as tightrope walkers and jugglers. Another fascinating clock of this time indicated the hours and minutes by means of a girl's arms rising and falling.

The blinking-eye clocks, which originated in the 17th century in Augsburg, were produced in simplified form in southern Germany in the mid 19th century and also in the United States. The latter were nearly all made of cast iron in the form of minstrels, dogs or lions.

Another series of ingenious clocks was made in France from around 1880 to 1910. These symbolized aspects of the Industrial Revolution and showed, for instance, a steam hammer or a steam engine at work, or a lighthouse revolving

MYSTERY, NOVELTY AND
FANTASY CLOCKS

The design of a 'swinger' means that in effect the whole clock is a pendulum. The movement is contained within the larger sphere at the top of the clock, while a smaller lead-filled sphere towards the bottom of the structure acts as a balance.

Clockmakers

Aaron D Crane, born in 1804, was an ingenious and self-taught clockmaker, who worked mainly in Newark, New Jersey. His main claim to fame was the invention of the torsion pendulum, which made possible the mass production of year-duration clocks in the hundreds of thousands, if not millions. Indeed, such clocks are still being made today (they are more popularly known as anniversary and 400-day clocks).

Silas B Terry, one of Eli Terry's sons, was an inventive clockmaker who designed a range of clocks with a variety of interesting movements.

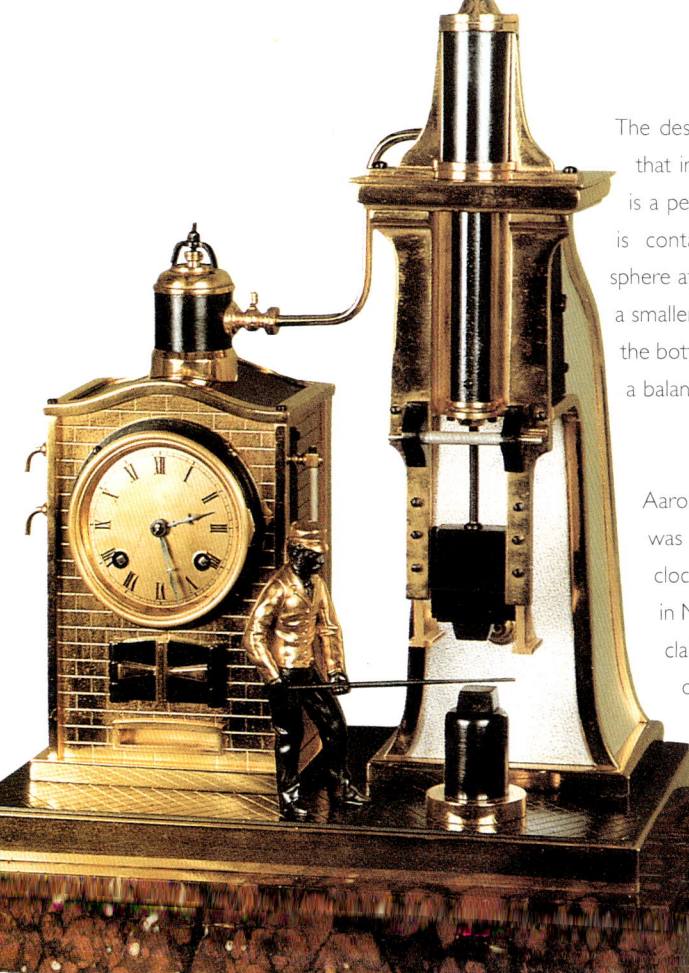

ABOVE This steam hammer clock is typical of those pieces made in France between 1870 to 1910 to symbolize aspects of the Industrial Revolution.

Swinging clocks

Swinging clocks, known as 'swingers', were produced in a variety of sizes in both France and the United States. The smallest examples often incorporated animals and made use of watch movements.

RIGHT The figure of Cupid holds the pendulum on this attractive French bronze swinging clock that dates from about 1880.

63

MYSTERY, NOVELTY AND
FANTASY CLOCKS

RIGHT This blinking-eye shelf clock is thought to be based on one of the characters from Lewis Carroll's Alice in Wonderland.

64